FunTime® Piano

Hits

Level 3A–3B

Easy Piano

Arranged by

Randall Faber and Jon Ophoff

Special Thanks to Christopher Oill
Editor: Isabel Otero Bowen
Design and Illustration: Terpstra Design, San Francisco
Engraving: Dovetree Productions, Inc.

FABER
PIANO ADVENTURES®
3042 Creek Drive
Ann Arbor, Michigan 48108

A NOTE TO TEACHERS

FunTime® Piano Hits is a collection of popular songs arranged for the Level 3 piano student. Enjoy blockbusters, chart-toppers, and award-winners as performed by stars such as Ed Sheeran, Lady Gaga, Justin Timberlake, and more.

FunTime® Piano Hits is part of the *FunTime Piano* series. "FunTime" designates Level 3 of the *PreTime to BigTime Piano Supplementary Library* arranged by Faber and Faber.

Following are the levels of the supplementary library, which lead from *PreTime to BigTime*.

PreTime® Piano	(Primer Level)
PlayTime® Piano	(Level 1)
ShowTime® Piano	(Level 2A)
ChordTime® Piano	(Level 2B)
FunTime® Piano	(Level 3A–3B)
BigTime® Piano	(Level 4)

Each level offers books in a variety of styles, making it possible for the teacher to offer stimulating material for every student. For a complimentary detailed listing, e-mail faber@pianoadventures.com or write us at the mailing address below.

Visit us at **PianoAdventures.com**.

Helpful Hints:

1. The songs can be assigned in any order. Selection is usually best made by the student, according to interest and enthusiasm.

2. As rhythm is of prime importance, encourage the student to feel the rhythm in his or her body when playing popular music. This can be accomplished with the tapping of the toe or heel, and with clapping exercises.

3. Identify chord names wherever possible (use both keyboard and score). For each measure having a change in harmony, write the chord symbol (G, Em, D7, etc.) above the staff, usually at beat 1. For support, see Piano Adventures® Scale & Chord Book 2, Section 7 on Chord Progressions and Harmony (FF3025).

ISBN 978-1-61677-695-4

TABLE OF CONTENTS

Love Yourself

Words and Music by JUSTIN BIEBER,
BENJAMIN LEVIN, ED SHEERAN,
JOSHUA GUDWIN and SCOTT BRAUN

Relaxed, in two (♩ = 88-100)

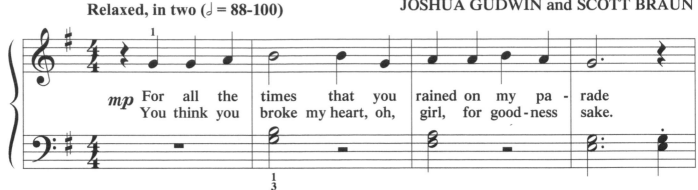

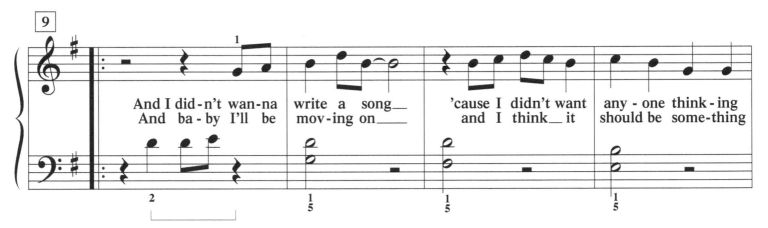

my ma-ma don't like you, and she likes ev-'ry-one.

And I ne-ver like to ad-mit that I was wrong.

And I've been so caught up in my job, did-n't

see what's go-ing on, and now I know,

I'm bet-ter sleep-ing on my own. 'Cause if you

like think the the that way I'm you still look that hold - ing much, on

oh, ba - by, to some - thing, you should go and love your - self.

1.

And if you

2.

mp

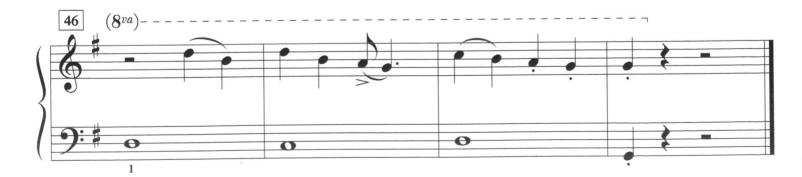

Feel It Still

Words and Music by
JOHN GOURLEY, ZACH CAROTHERS, JASON SECHRIST, ERIC HOWK,
KYLE O'QUIN, BRIAN HOLLAND, FREDDIE GORMAN, GEORGIA DOBBINS,
ROBERT BATEMAN, WILLIAM GARRETT, JOHN HILL and ASA TACCONE

Fast rock (♩ = 138–160)

FF3036

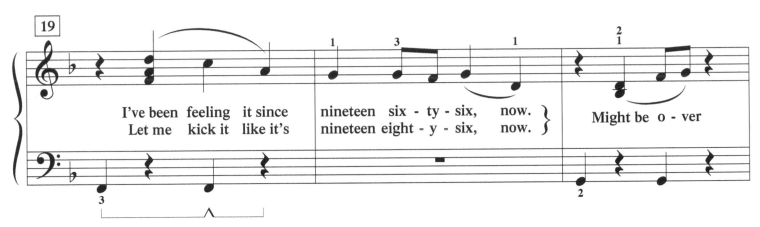

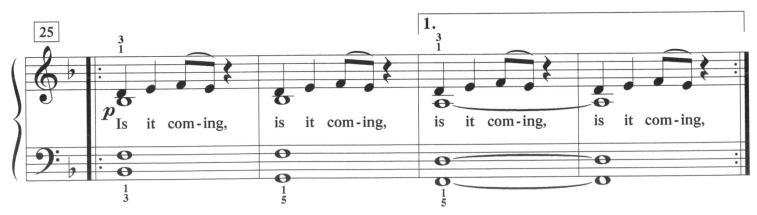

2.

R.H. 2

L.H. over

f *p*

back? Ooh,_____ I'm a

reb - el just for kicks. Your love is an a - byss for my heart to e - clipse, now.

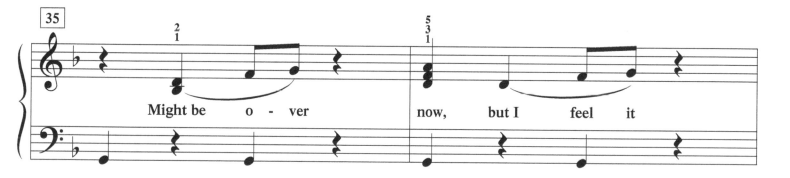

Might be o - ver now, but I feel it

D.S. al Coda

still.

⊕ *Coda*

Might have had your fill, but you feel it still.___

Million Reasons

Words and Music by STEFANI GERMANOTTA,
MARK RONSON, and HILLARY LINDSEY

Steady ballad (♩ = 60-66)

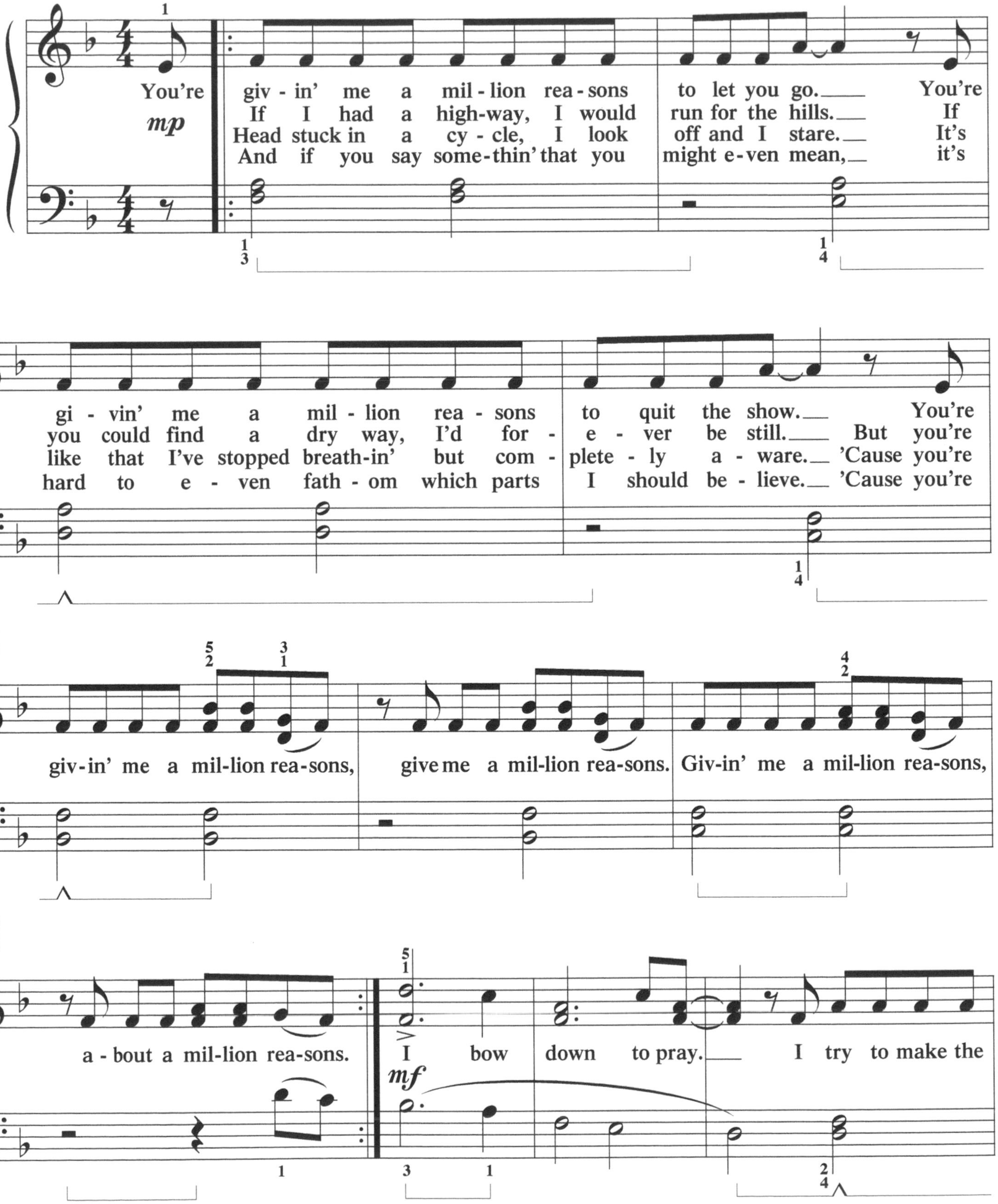

Lyrics under the staves:

You're giv-in' me a mil-lion rea-sons to let you go.___ You're
If I had a high-way, I would run for the hills.___ If
Head stuck in a cy-cle, I look off and I stare.___ It's
And if you say some-thin' that you might e-ven mean,___ it's

gi-vin' me a mil-lion rea-sons to quit the show.___ You're
you could find a dry way, I'd for-ev-er be still.___ But you're
like that I've stopped breath-in' but com-plete-ly a-ware.___ 'Cause you're
hard to e-ven fath-om which parts I should be-lieve.___ 'Cause you're

giv-in' me a mil-lion rea-sons, give me a mil-lion rea-sons. Giv-in' me a mil-lion rea-sons,

a-bout a mil-lion rea-sons. I bow down to pray.___ I try to make the

Treat You Better

Driving, not too fast (♩ = 144-160)

Words and Music by SHAWN MENDES,
SCOTT HARRIS, and TEDDY GEIGER

be with me _____ in - stead. I know I can treat you _____

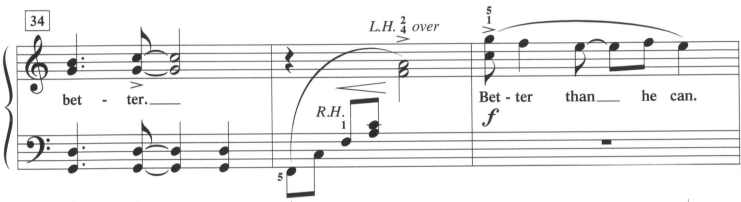

bet - ter. _____ Bet - ter than _____ he can.

Bet - ter than _____ he can.

Bet - ter than _____ he can.

Lost Boy

Words and Music by
RUTH BERHE

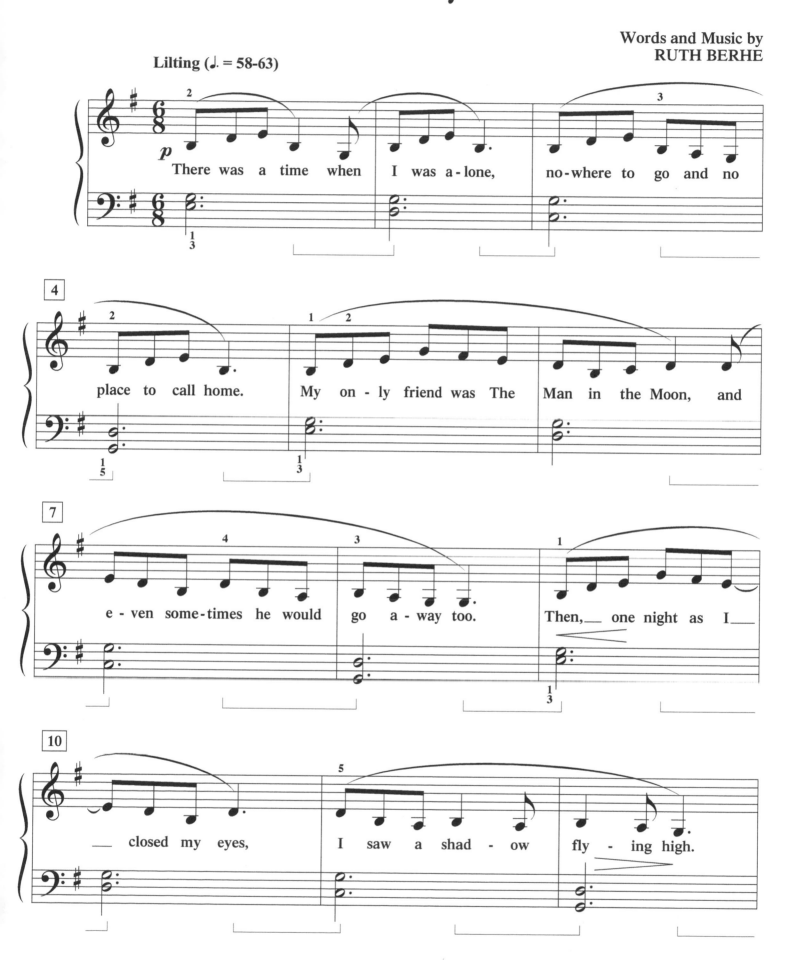

FF3036

FF3036

Fight Song

Words and Music by RACHEL PLATTEN
and DAVE BASSETT

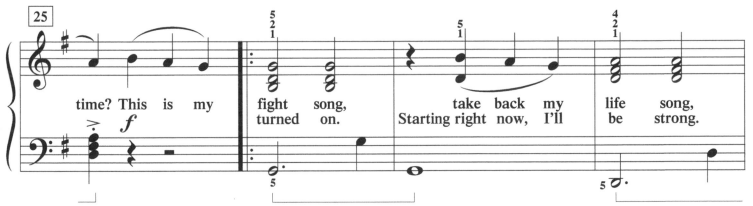

Photograph

Words and Music by ED SHEERAN, JOHNNY McDAID,
MARTIN PETER HARRINGTON and TOM LEONARD

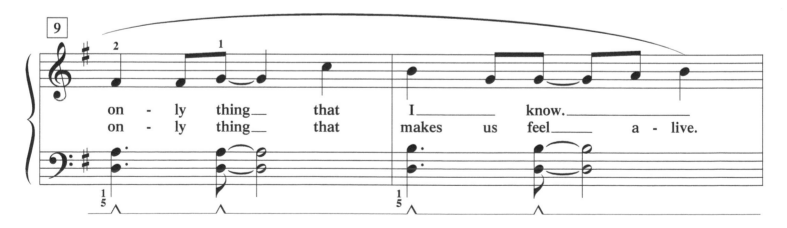

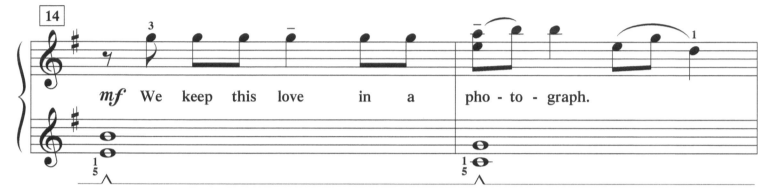

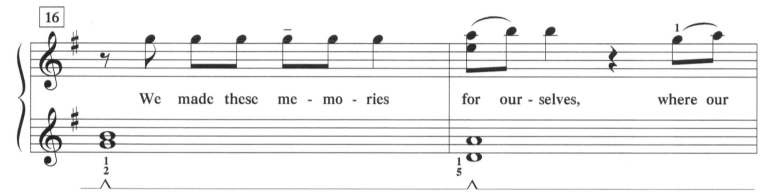

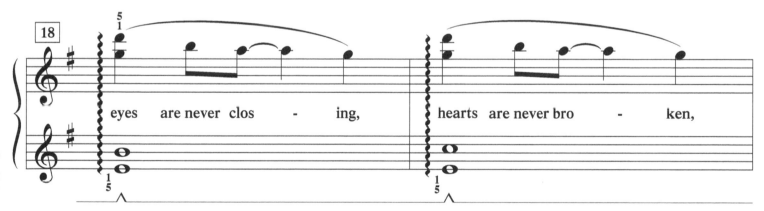

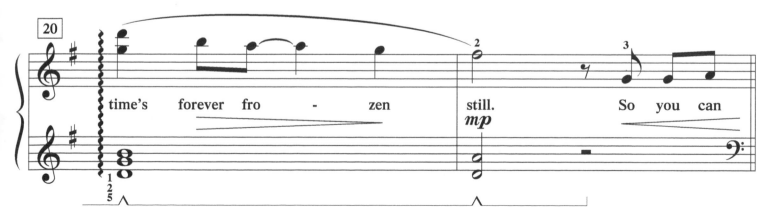

keep me in - side the pock - et of your ripped jeans,

mf

hold - in' me clos - er 'til our eyes meet.

You won't e - ver be a - lone.

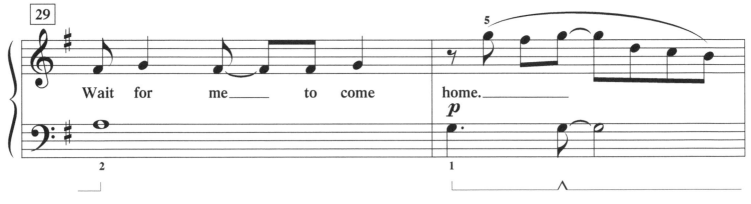

Wait for me___ to come home.___

p

rit.

Roar

Words and Music by
KATY PERRY, MAX MARTIN, DR. LUKE,
BONNIE McKEE, and HENRY WALTER

Rocking, with swing (♩ = 160-184)

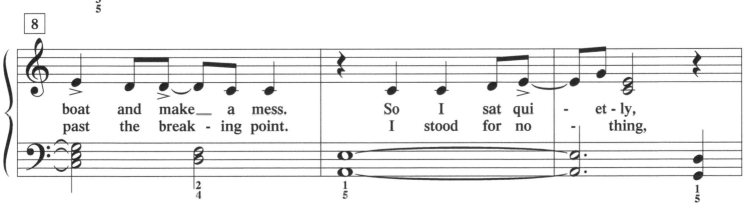

Lyrics:
I used to bite my tongue and hold__ my breath.
I guess I for-got I had__ a choice.
Scared to rock the boat and make__ a mess.
I let you push me past the break-ing point.
So I sat qui-et-ly, I stood for no-thing,
a-greed po-lite-ly.
so I fell for ev-'ry-thing.
You

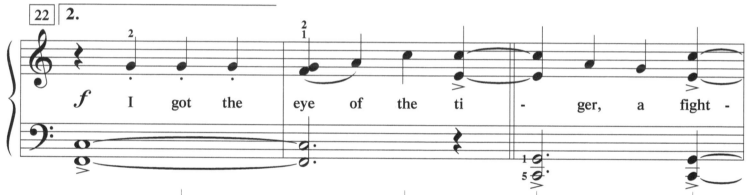

er, loud - er than the li - on, 'cause I_____ am a champ -

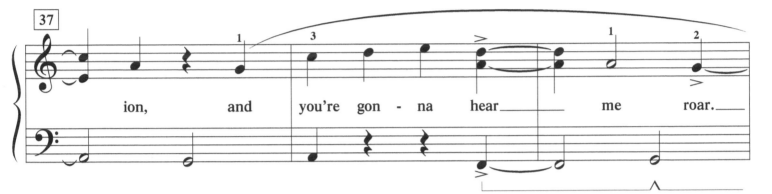

ion, and you're gon - na hear_____ me roar._____

Oh - oh - oh, oh, oh, oh, oh - oh - oh. Oh - oh - oh, oh,

oh, oh, oh - oh - oh. Oh - oh - oh, oh, oh, oh, oh - oh - oh.

You're gon - na hear_____ me_____ roar._____

Radioactive

Words and Music by DANIEL REYNOLDS,
BENJAMIN McKEE, DANIEL SERMON,
ALEXANDER GRANT and JOSH MOSSER

Moderate rock (♩ = 126–138)

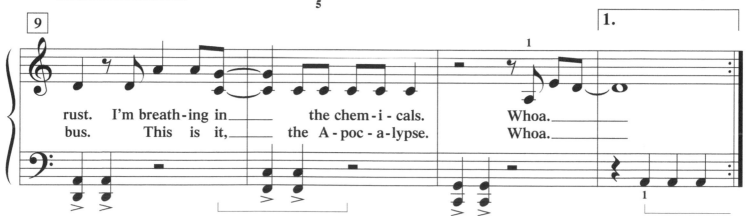

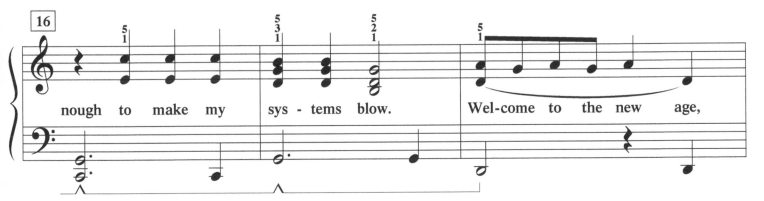

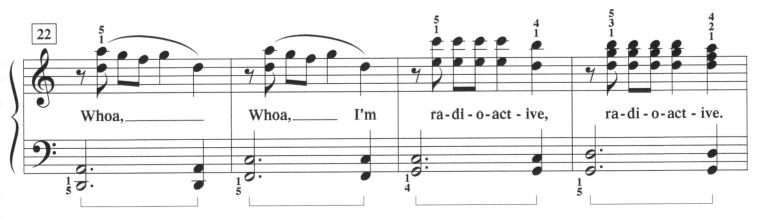

from the Summit Entertainment film *The Twilight Saga: Breaking Dawn - Part 1*

A Thousand Years

Words and Music by DAVID HODGES
and CHRISTINA PERRI

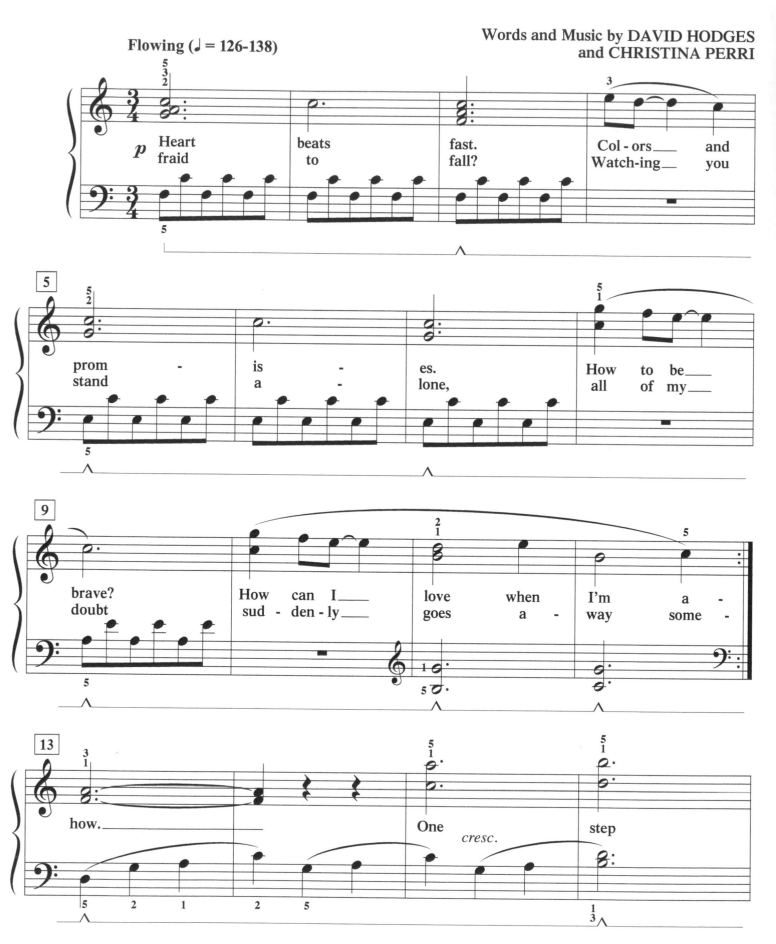

from *Trolls*

Can't Stop the Feeling

Words and Music by JUSTIN TIMBERLAKE,
MAX MARTIN and SHELLBACK

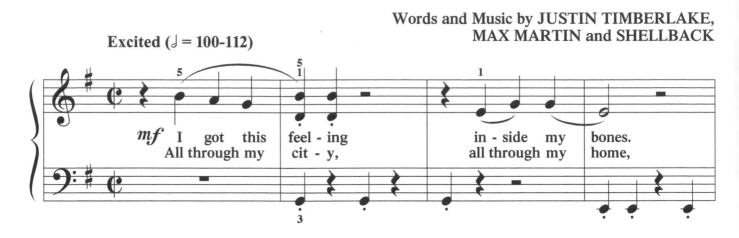

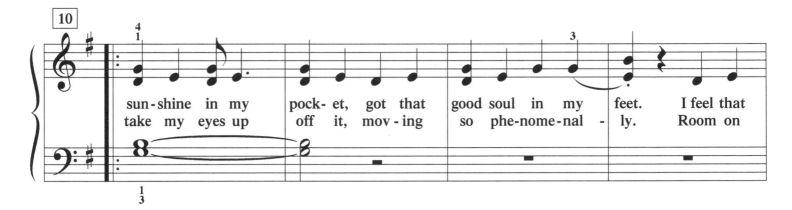

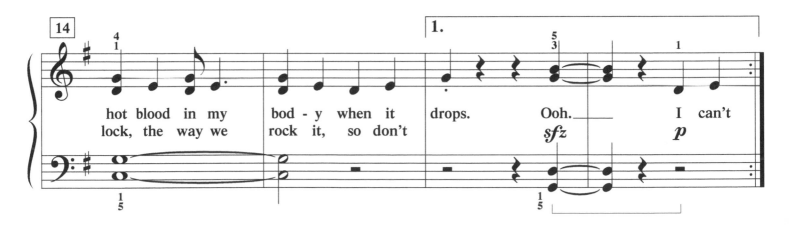

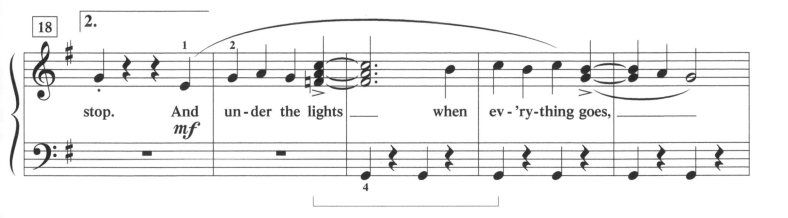

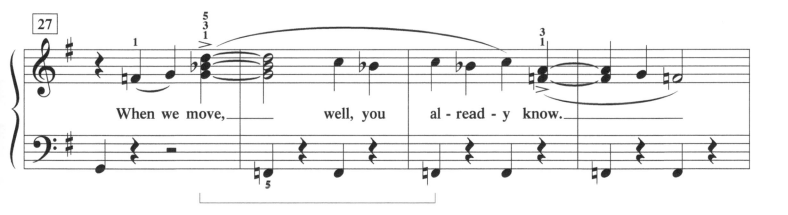

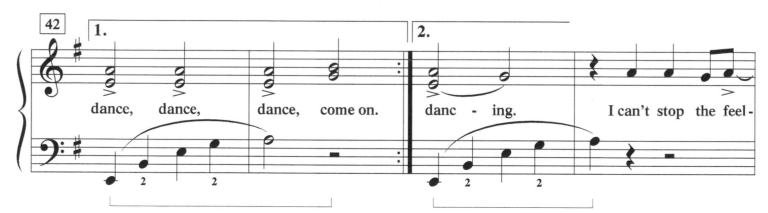